HOLY HUMOR

SUNDAY
SMILES

Publications International, Ltd.

Front Cover: Shutterstock.com

Back Cover: Jonny Hawkins

Contributing Author: When not sitting in church praying for inspiration and taking notes for holy humor books, Paul Seaburn is the head writer for *12th Street Jump*, a jazz-blues-and-comedy show on public radio and writes scripts for many Internet comedy video providers. Check out his latest musings on Facebook.

Cartoonist: Jonny Hawkins, the son of a former pastor and his pianist wife, began drawing cartoons in church while his dad was preaching. In Bible college in 1986, he sold his first to a Sunday School newsletter ... and has been selling them ever since. His work has appeared in *Reader's Digest, National Catholic Register, Guideposts, Parade, Focus on the Family, Woman's World,* in 77 *Chicken Soup for the Soul* titles and in over 600 other publications. He lives with his wife, Carissa, and their three children near his boyhood home in Sherwood, MI.

Additional Illustrations: Art Explosion, Shutterstock.com, Jamie Smith, Jan Smith

Louis Weber, CEO
Publications International, Ltd.
7373 North Cicero Avenue
Lincolnwood, Illinois 60712

Permission is never granted for commercial purposes.

ISBN-13: 978-1-4508-7823-4
ISBN-10: 1-4508-7823-7

Manufactured in U.S.A.

8 7 6 5 4 3 2 1

Whether you read them on Sunday or any other day of the week, these cartoons and stories about church, faith, and God will tickle your funny bone and send your giggles, chuckles, and belly laughs heavenward.

Three rival pastors decided to hold a secret contest to see who could recruit the most new members in a month. They each bet $100 with the winner taking all. Thirty days later, they got back together to see who won.

"I recruited 50 new members," said the first pastor as he held out his hand for the money.

"Not so fast," said the second, "I recruited 50 new members too! We should have picked a tiebreaker!"

"Don't worry about it," said the third pastor as he smiled and handed each a 50-dollar bill. "I LOST 100 members."

"So why are you smiling?" the first pastor asked.

The losing pastor grinned even wider. "None of them have tithed in years."

***

Dear Pastor,
I'm sorry I couldn't leave more money in the plate. Could you please have a sermon about a raise in my allowance?

Stephanie, age 10

***

After Sunday school, Marcus reported to his parents, "Syntax is all the money collected at the church from sinners."

Lisa came home from Sunday school and told her mother that she had learned a new song about a cross-eyed bear named Gladly. It took her mother awhile before she realized that the hymn was really "Gladly the Cross I'd Bear."

***

Flowers for Sunday's services were donated by Smith Chrysler Plymouth. Mrs. Smith will also be the choir's guest soloist, singing "A Mighty Fortress Is Our Dodge."

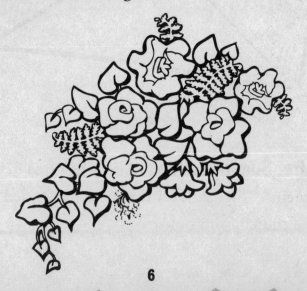

The Meteorologist's Hymn:

"There Shall Be Showers of Blessings"

***

The Optometrist's Hymn:

"Open My Eyes That I Might See Thee"

***

The Dentist's Hymn:

"Crown Him with Many Crowns"

***

The Golfer's Hymn:

"There's a Green Hill Far Away"

***

The SUV Bible

Dear God,
I would like to know why in the Bible all the things you said are in red?

Joanne, age 8

***

Josh was trying to teach his puppy to walk alongside him by reading the Bible to him. When asked why, he said, "I'm using the heeling power of prayer."

Bulletin Bloopers

Our soloist has returned from having reconstructive surgery. The choir is happy to welcome her back with a joyful nose.

***

The church will host an evening of fine dining, superb entertainment, and gracious hostility.

The outreach committee has enlisted 25 visitors to call on people who are not already afflicted with another church.

✳✳✳

We now have a Lost & Found. If you have lost anything, please place it in the big, green box in the administrative office.

Although she didn't have a cold, little Susie was constantly blowing her nose into tissues during the church service. After some loud honking, Sally would wad up the tissue and place it carefully next to her on the pew. Then she would stare at it intently. After a few minutes, she would scratch her head and start the process all over again.

When it appeared she was disturbing the other churchgoers, her mom whispered for her to stop and asked why she was staring at all of those wadded tissues. "I'm waiting for God to do what the preacher said he would do," Susie said.

"What's that?" asked her mom.

Sally replied, "He said that Our Father would lead a snot into temptation."

***

The Sunday school teacher asked Sarah why she drew Jesus sitting on a horse. Sarah replied, "He's giving his sermon on the mount."

***

Amanda explained why she brought her dolls to Sunday school: "I'm building a Tower of Barbie."

***

Some Children's Prayers

Now I lay me down to rest,
I hope I pass tomorrow's test.
If I should die before I wake,
That's one less test I have to take.

Amen

Dear God,

Please take care of Daddy and Mommy and my sister and my brother and me. And please take care of yourself, God. If anything happens to you, we're gonna be in a big mess.

Dear God,
I don't think anybody could be a better God. I just wanted you to know that. And I am not just saying that because you are God already.

Bobby, age 4

***

Lord,

If you can't make me a better boy, don't worry about it. I'm having a real good time just as I am.

"IT'S NOT THE HEAT, IT'S THE HUMILITY."

Over the massive front doors of a church, these words were inscribed: "The Gates of Heaven." Below that was a small cardboard sign saying, "Please use basement entrance."

***

We pray that our people will jumble themselves before God.

***

A priest, a rabbi, and a minister were discussing the best time of the day to pray. "I like to pray in the morning when I hear the sound of the birds chirping," said the priest.

"I like to pray late at night when I hear the sound of the owls hooting," said the rabbi.

"The time of the day doesn't matter to me," said the minister. "I like to pray when I hear the sound of my neighbor saying, 'Hey, Harry! Watch this!'"

***

My pastor says you must love your neighbor, even if you hate him.

***

If you, or someone close to you, are challenged by illness and are having a difficult time coping, please join our support group. Meetings are Thursday evenings at 7:00 in the back room of The Old Towne Pub.

✱✱✱

We need one more player on the church soccer team. Ask yourself: "Am I my brother's goalkeeper?"

✱✱✱

"WE'RE LEARNING THAT WE ARE THE CHURCH
... AND THOSE ARE OUR STEEPLE PEOPLE."

We have been experiencing some problems with our church elevator. If it stops between floors, do not become alarmed. Simply press the "Alarm" button, and we will contact a maintenance person.

***

We continue to apologize for our broken air conditioner. Please join us for hot coffee and toasted bagels immediately following the services.

***

Three little boys were having a discussion about what they planned to take with them when they finally get to heaven.

"I'm taking my trombone," said Peter. "I want to get into the heavenly band and everybody else will be playing harps so I'll have no competition." The other two boys thought that was a good idea.

"I'm taking a car," said James. "Everybody else will be flying around with their wings so there will be no one else on the roads." The other boys thought that was a good idea too.

"I'm bringing some beans," said John. The other boys couldn't figure out why. "I want to get on God's good side and I know he likes beans because he's our Father who farts in heaven."

***

Emily was having a little difficulty with the Lord's Prayer: "Our Father, who does art in heaven...."

***

A six-year-old was overheard reciting the Lord's Prayer in church: "And forgive us our trash passes, as we forgive those who passed trash against us."

***

Dear Pastor,
I think a lot more people would probably come to your church if you moved it to Disneyland.

Lauren, age 9

***

The pastor will preach his farewell message, after which the choir will sing, "Joy, Joy, Joy."

Dear Pastor,
Please say in your sermon that Jimmy Patterson has been a good boy all week. I am Jimmy Patterson.

Jimmy, age 7

***

Dear Pastor,
Could you please say a prayer
for our Little League team?
We either need God's help
or a new pitcher.

Tim, age 11

"CHECKIN' FOR CELL PHONES."

We knew Reverend Smith was irritated by interruptions when he said, "In I Corinthians 7:20 we read: 'Let every man abide in the same calling wherein he was called'—except on his cell phone in church!"

***

Preacher Tina quoted Job 5:1: "Call now, if there be any that will answer thee."

A voice in the back of the church replied, "Operators are standing by."

***

Little Johnny's Sunday school teacher asked what his favorite Bible story was. He said it was the one about the lady who was a bad driver. The puzzled teacher wasn't familiar with the story, so he asked Johnny to tell it.

"There was a big snow storm coming," Johnny began, "so Lot decided to get a delivery of rock salt. He didn't have any bags so he used whatever he could find to hold it, including some stuff from the bedroom. He had almost all of it stacked in the back of the garage when his wife came home. She was talking on her cell phone and didn't pay attention when she made a hard right into the garage. And that's how Lot's wife turned into a pillow of salt."

***

After Sunday school Nathan asked his mom, "Why would Jesus want 12 opossums?"

***

"Why did Moses have to go back up the mountain a second time?" asked the Sunday school teacher.

"To ask God for a map," Brad replied.

***

"IT'S A COMBINATION BIRD BATH
AND BAPTISTRY."

Baptismal pool repairs have been postponed for a week because Reverend Atkins has been feeling under the water.

***

Reverend Vicky was asked to perform some baptisms for a traveling circus, so she took the clowns down to the river for a fool immersion.

***

When Father Steve was working on his Sunday sermon, he often took a break and went out to dinner at his favorite restaurant, hoping a good meal would inspire him. For the second week in a row, his waitress was one of his parishioners. He explained to her why he was there and asked if she had any advice.

"Why don't you do the same thing you did to get your inspiration for last week's sermon," she told him. "Go to the men's room, wash your hands of all of the things that are blocking your thought process, and then push the button and hold them under the hot air."

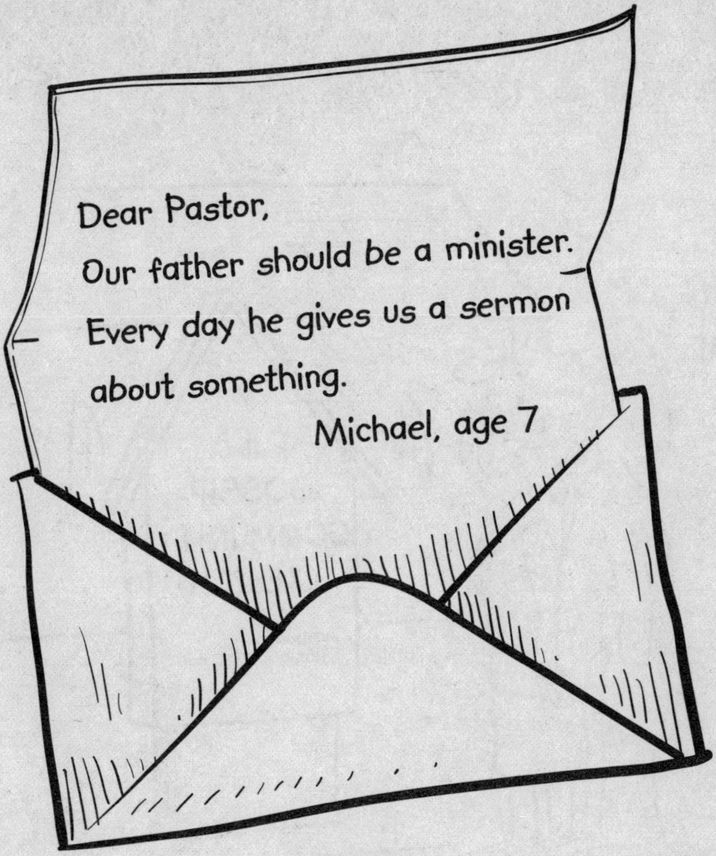

Dear Pastor,
Our father should be a minister.
Every day he gives us a sermon
about something.

Michael, age 7

***

Reverend Nichols must have known what
effect his long sermons were having on the
congregation when he accidentally referred to
them as "bored-again Christians."

"IT'S QUITE AN ACTIVE CHURCH... AT LEAST
THAT'S WHAT I'VE HEARD."

THE MORNING SERMON:

Gossip...The Speaking of Evil

THE EVENING SERMON:

I Love to Tell the Story

***

Thursday night:

Potluck dinner.
Prayer and medication to follow.

***

Bulletin Bloopers

This evening at 7:00 there will be a hymn sing in the park across from the church. Bring a blanket and come prepared to sin.

***

The visiting monster is Reverend Jack Bains.

The concert held in Fellowship Hall was a great success. Special thanks are due to the minister's daughter, who labored the whole evening at the piano, which as usual fell on her.

***

"I'LL COME OUT AND PLAY IN A MINUTE.
I'M HAVING A TEACHABLE MOMENT."

Dear God,
I read the Bible. What does "begat" mean? Nobody will tell me.

Alison, age 9

***

"I think the richest animal is the mink," Lisa told her best friend. "I heard in church that the mink shall inherit the earth."

Reverend Hank decided to spend his day off fishing. When he arrived at his favorite lake, he was surprised to find Joe, a member of his congregation who was known to sleep through most of the service. The fish must have been biting because Joe already had three nice bass in his bucket.

Reverend Hank asked Joe what he was using for bait.

"I followed the advice you gave last Sunday," Joe told him. "I got three worms and named them Keith Richards, Charlie Watts, and Ron Wood. Every one of them caught a fish."

Figuring Joe must have been asleep and dreaming, Reverend Hank asked why Joe didn't use a worm named Mick Jagger.

"Mick was the founder of the band and I'm not the greatest at following the Commandments," Joe told Hank. "And you said that only he who was without sin could cast the first Stone."

"Let's sing that hymn about fishing," Pat told his Sunday school teacher. "You know, 'He's Got the Whole Worm in His Hands.'"

***

After today's services, the choir will meet in the rehearsal room next to the restrooms to practice a new hymn: "Who Is He in Yonder Stall?"

***

The old church pipe organ had seen better days. After one particularly out-of-tune song, the pastor turned to his assistant and said, "I don't know if we need an organ tuner or a plumber."

***

For all of his religious life, the minister supported the constitutional separation of church and state. After one particularly bad month when he couldn't afford to pay his church's bills, he decided to change his mind. He traveled to Washington and explained his problem to his congressman.

The congressman told him that the Constitution prevented him from giving his church financial help.

"I'm not asking the government for money," replied the minister. "I'm just asking you to tell the Federal Reserve to stop printing ones and fives."

***

Next Sunday a special collection will be taken to defray the cost of the new carpet. All those wishing to do something on the new carpet will come forward and do so at that time.

***

Remember the youth department rummage sale to raise funds for summer camp. We have a Gents three-speed bicycle, also two ladies for sale, in good running order.

***

SOMEWHERE IN THE USHER
PREPARATION CLASS, THERE WAS
A COMMUNICATION BREAKDOWN.

If all of the pews are full when you arrive, please wait in the aisle for help from one of the pushers.

***

Offertory hymn:

"Jesus Paid It All!"

***

Little Lucy's parents brought their five-year-old purple-haired daughter to their minister's office. "This is all your fault," the angry father told the minister as he pointed to his daughter's hair, which had a few of her original blonde roots showing.

"How on earth is this my fault?" the minister asked.

"In your sermon Sunday, you talked about how wonderful heaven is," the father said. "And then you said you couldn't understand why people weren't just dying to get there."

***

After Bobby's pet bird died, he decided it needed a proper funeral. He held a wonderful service in the backyard and concluded with, "Ashes to ashes, ducks to ducks."

***

"MAY I HAVE A WORD WITH YOU ABOUT
THE NEW SPRING CHOIR OUTFITS?"

The congregation will sing "Savior, Like a Shepherd Lead Us"…if time permits.

***

Next Sunday, Mrs. Benson will be soloist for the morning service. The pastor will then speak on "Hell on Earth."

Some Children's Prayers

Dear God,

I think the stapler is one of your greatest inventions.

Ruth, age 10

Dear God,
I would like to live 900 years
like that guy in the Bible.

Jason, age 9

Dear God,

My brother is a rat. You should give him a tail.

Patrick, age 7

***

Dear God,

I think about you sometimes, even when I'm not praying.

Henry, age 4

Reverend Jerry was a former radio disc jockey who sometimes liked to use his old radio promotions to stir up the congregation. This week, he advertised an "All Request Sunday" and promised that the tenth person to yell "Amen" would get to pick three songs for the choir to sing.

He counted down the "Amens" and the tenth one came from a lovely young woman whom he had never seen before. Pleased that his promotion brought in a new member, he brought her to the front of the church and told her to pick out her three hymns. The young lady got a sly grin on her face, turned to the all-male choir, and said, "I'll take him, him, and him!"

***

Young Adult Weekend.

All singles are invited to spend
a weekend in the presence
of the Lord and other
interesting singles.

***

The church bowling team is looking for players. All skill levels welcome. Come join us even if you're in the gutter.

***

"LOVE, HONOR, AND CHERISH? YOU
DRIVE A HARD BARGAIN."

A little boy was attending his first wedding. After the service, his cousin asked him, "How many women can a man marry?"

"Sixteen," the boy responded.

His cousin was amazed that he had an answer so quickly. "How do you know that?" he asked.

"Easy," the little boy said. "All you have to do is add it up, like the pastor said: four better, four worse, four richer, four poorer."

"SHE'S WORKING IN THE NURSERY TODAY."

Bouncing out of her first day at nursery school, a three-year-old girl gleefully informed her mother, "We had juice and Billy Graham crackers!"

***

A Sunday school teacher asked his class why Joseph and Mary took Jesus with them to Jerusalem. One confident child replied, "They couldn't get a babysitter."

***

The minister was passing out "What Would Jesus Do?" bumper stickers to his congregation. Everyone took at least one except for Louie.

"Why don't you want a WWJD bumper sticker for your car, Louie?" the minister asked.

"I'm a New York taxi driver," Louie told him. "If I put this on my cab, I'll have to quit my job."

***

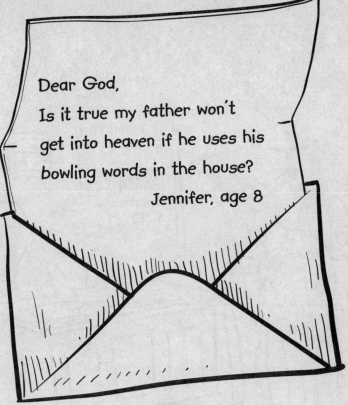

Dear God,
Is it true my father won't get into heaven if he uses his bowling words in the house?

Jennifer, age 8

***

Dear God,
It rained our whole vacation and, boy, was my father mad. He said some things about you that people are not supposed to say, but I hope you do not hurt him anyway.

Anna, age 4

"WE'RE FROM THE POLICE DEPARTMENT
EXPLOSIVES UNIT. WE HAVE REASON
TO BELIEVE THAT YOUR SERMON
ON SUNDAY WILL BOMB."

Before viewing slides from the pastor's recent conference, the choir will sing "O God, We Ask for Strength."

***

Hymn 43: "Great God, What Do I Hear?"
Preacher: The Rev. Mark Mahoney
Hymn 47: "Hark! An Awful Voice Is Sounding."

Bulletin Bloopers

Our guest speaker is a prison minister who will talk about Christian felonship.

***

After eating Christmas dinner, join us in the church hall for a Christmas concert. The choir will open with "O Come All Ye Facefull."

The vote to turn off the heat during the week to save gas has been passed.

***

Sunday worship will begin with personal medication.

***

66

Dear God,
I bet it is very hard for you to love everybody in the whole world. There are only four people in our family, and I can never do it.

Julie, age 8

***

Dear God,
We had a good time at church today. Wish you could have been there.

Matthew, age 7

Sally and her grandpa were looking through one of her Bible picture books and having a talk about heaven. "I'll probably be going to heaven before you," Grandpa told Sally. "Is there anything you want me to tell Jesus for you?"

She looked down at the book and nodded her head. "There's one thing I want you to tell him, but don't hurt his feelings."

"I don't think that will happen, honey," Grandpa told her. "What do you want me to tell Jesus for you?"

Sally pointed to a picture of Jesus and put her finger on his head. "Tell him those big yellow round things aren't hats," she whispered. "They're Frisbees!"

***

"Grandpa should have been in the Garden of Eden instead of Adam," Jules told his mom.

"Why do you think that?" asked his mom.

Jules answered, "Because he can't eat an apple without his false teeth."

***

"HEAVEN'S STREETS ARE PAVED
WITH GOLD? I WAS REALLY
HOPING FOR CHOCOLATE."

A rich man was looking for a loophole in the "You can't take it with you" rule and thought he figured it out. He had his gold melted and stored in jugs marked "holy water." When he died, his family followed his instructions and had him buried with the jugs.

Lo and behold, when he arrived in heaven, he found that the jugs were there with him. "We've been waiting for a smart guy like you," St. Peter told him. "Grab those jugs and start filling the potholes in the street."

To teach the students the power of prayer, the Sunday school teacher asked the class, "What does the Bible tell you to do before making a decision?"

"Check with Bernie," replied little Joey.

"Who is Bernie?" asked the teacher.

"He's the guy Moses got his instructions from," explained Joey. "Bernie Bush."

***

Little Johnny was crying on his way home from church. His father repeatedly asked him what was wrong. Johnny finally replied, "The preacher said he wanted us brought up in a Christian home, but I want to stay with you guys!"

***

Mickey told his mom he was afraid the pastor would throw an egg at him because he said in the sermon: "Take my yoke upon you."

***

"WE'RE HAVING A FISH FRY ON FRIDAY,
AND SUNDAY AFTER THE SERVICE WE'RE
ROASTING THE PREACHER."

Before sending shipments of bottled water to people who have not yet found God, Reverend Peter will pray for their salivation.

***

Reverend Ryan was definitely on a diet when he said, "Be good, low-carb Christians and do not partake of the forbidden fruits."

***

The first question on the Bible studies test was, "What was Jesus' occupation?" The teacher found "Jesus was a carpenter" on every test until she got to Freddy's.

He wrote, "Jesus brought toilet paper to his customers in Galilee on horseback."

Not knowing that Bible story, she made a red X next to the answer. When handing the tests back, she asked Freddy to explain.

"You told us yourself," he answered. "You said Jesus delivered his Charmin on the mount in Galilee."

***

While sitting in church on Sunday morning, Sally's dad noticed she was holding his favorite coffee mug — the one with the broken handle that never seemed to stay glued. He asked Sally quietly why she brought the broken mug to church.

"I heard what the minister said last week," she told her dad. "What God has joined together, no man can separate."

***

"IT'S NOT MY POSSE, LENNY...
IT'S CALLED A CHOIR."

Miss Charlene Mason sang "I Will Not Pass This Way Again," which brought great joy to the congregation.

***

"I'm pleased to report we finally found a plumber for the church washroom," Reverend Wes told the congregation. "And now, let us sing: 'O Happy Day.'"

***

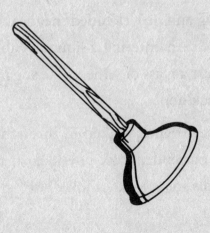

After a long day of performing his religious duties, Father Ray decided he deserved to reward himself with one glass of wine. Not wanting to be seen drinking alone, he called up his old friend, Rabbi Wayne.

The rabbi had also put in a long day and was feeling the same way. He was concerned that some of his flock might see the two men together and get the wrong idea, so he suggested they invite their mutual friend, Reverend Chuck, to join them.

The minister was just finishing a long day of ministering and he welcomed the idea, but didn't want to be seen entering a liquor establishment, even for just a glass of wine, so he suggested they use the back door.

As the three friends walked in through the back door, the bartender took one look at them and said, "Is this some kind of joke?"

To help her students understand and accept all faiths, the religion teacher asked each one to pick a religion, study it carefully, and give a report on at least one thing they liked about that religion.

Every student did the research and all of them found something of interest in each religion, except Johnny. "I could never become a Quaker,"he told the teacher. "I hate oatmeal."

***

"YOUR SERMON MADE 'EM ITCH, PASTOR,
AND HERE'S THE SCRATCH."

This week our church will be collecting the following items: kitchen matches and school textbooks.

***

Please put your donation along with any suggestions in the correction basket.

***

The Sunday school teacher asked, "Now Thomas, tell me frankly, do you say a prayer before eating?"

"No, sir," Thomas replied, "I don't have to. My mom is a good cook."

***

Dear God,
I want to be just like my Daddy when I get big, but with not so much hair all over.

Sam, age 8

Asked to recite the Ten Commandments, Tommy said, "Well, I don't remember the first four, but the Fifth Commandment is humor thy father and mother."

***

"YOUR TIE IS RATHER LOUD
TODAY, PASTOR."

The new minister was having a tough time preaching the Bible to the members of his church, most of whom were highly paid investment bankers. Hoping to get them to read it, he opened his sermon with the following question: "'It is easier for a camel to go through the eye of a needle than for a rich man to enter the kingdom of God.' Does anyone here know where in the Bible you can find this advice?"

Immediately everyone in the church raised their hands and waved them excitedly.

He pointed to a well-dressed man in the front row who jumped up and yelled, "Chapter 11."

All day long, the little boy sat in front of the exit door of a store. Finally, the store manager became worried so he went to talk to him. "What are you doing here?" he asked the boy.

"I'm waiting for Jesus," the boy replied.

"How do you know he's coming here?" the manager asked the boy.

"I heard it in church," he explained. "Jesus will be coming through the OUT door because the preacher said there's no room at the IN."

When Jimmy's mother asked him what he had learned in Sunday school, Jimmy replied, "Jesus was big on the golden rule, which says to do one to others before they do one to you."

***

Dear God,
I hope to go to heaven someday, but later rather than sooner.

Logan, age 5

"IT'S HIS WAY OF INSTANT MESSAGING."

Reverend Bill had to stop the teen Bible class and explain to one young computer whiz that Emmanuel is not an online instruction guide you get when you buy a new PC.

✳✳✳

Deacon Steve is our church's Internet preacher. His sermons always have references to e-commerce, e-mail, and e-pistles.

✳✳✳

Today's blessing of the pets will be followed by the "Sermon on the Mouse."

***

The pastor welcomes you to the blessing of the pets. He will greet you in the church barking lot.

***

We will have a blessing of the pets after the 9:00 service. Dogs and cats first, other animals blessed after. Please keep birds, reptiles, rodents, and fish separrot.

***

94

Bob was frantic. He looked everywhere and could not find his car keys. He spent an hour tearing the house apart and they were nowhere to be found. Finally, he decided to pray. "God, if you help me find my car keys, I'll drive to church every Sunday, give rides to little old ladies, and never speed again."

Just then he looked down and there were the keys. He smiled, looked up and said, "Never mind—here they are!"

The priest was telling telling the story of Jonah in his sermon in order to illustrate that we should be grateful for God's care just like Jonah was grateful that God freed him from the belly of the giant fish. As the churchgoers filed out after Mass, he asked one little boy if he knew why Jonah was grateful.

"Sure, Father," said the boy. "Jonah was grateful because God got him out of that fish before someone caught it and ate it on Friday!"

***

After the service, Johnny asked his mother, "In the preacher's sermon on Acts today he said the apostles were all in one Accord. Did they really have cars back then?"

***

"There are girl angels," May told her brother. "Their names are Cher Ubim and Sarah Phim."

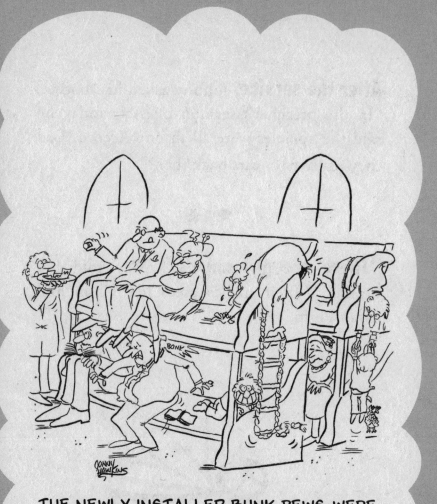

THE NEWLY INSTALLED BUNK PEWS WERE
THE ANSWER TO MOUNTAIN VALLEY'S
RAPID GROWTH, THOUGH THEY TOOK A
LITTLE GETTING USED TO.

Brian's father asked him what he really liked about church. Brian thought about it a moment and replied, "The benediction."

***

The congregation is asked to remain seated until the end of the recession.

Bulletin Bloopers

Ladies' Bible Study will be held on Thursday at 10:00 in the morning. All ladies are invited to lunch in the Fellowship Hall after the B.S. is over.

***

Following the minister's return to health from illness: "GOD IS GOOD! Dr. Harmon is better."

***

A Teen Dance Social will be held in the gym next Friday evening at 7:30. All teenagers must be at least 13 years old.

***

Our pastor will be attending a week long seminar on mental illnesses. Please pray for his sane return.

***

"I FOUND YOUR SERMON ON THE
END TIMES INTERESTING."

"What is Armageddon?" Wanda asked her father.

"That's where the Messiah will come back to earth and do battle with the Antichrist and Satan until he kills them," replied her dad.

"What's he going to kill them with?" she asked.

"Swords and fire and lightning bolts and bombs, I guess," he told her.

"Well, if he's the Messiah, why doesn't he kill them with kindness?" she asked.

"Because," he explained, "Then it would have to be called the Charmageddon."

Reverend Zeke was probably thinking about his fishing trip that afternoon when he said in his sermon: "Let them have dominion over the fish of the sea, and the lake and the river and the pond too."

***

"These kids see way too many movies," one Sunday school teacher told another. "Now they think Jonah should have been saved from the whale by Nemo."

***

Dear God,

The bad people laughed at Noah and said, "You made an ark on dry land, silly." But Noah was smart and he stuck with you. That's what I would do.

William, age 7

***

"HONESTLY, HONEY! – FOR ONE VACATION, CAN'T YOU LEAVE YOUR MINISTRY HOME?!"

Dear God,
In Sunday school they told us
what you do. But who does it
when you are on vacation?

Jill, age 10

***

"Yes, Joseph and Mary were traveling to Nazareth," Reverend Martin responded to a question from a young man in his Bible study class, "but I don't think they would have called it a weekend getaway."

The pastor of a small church went visiting the homes in his area looking to recruit new members. At one house, he met a man he'd never seen before. He said to him, "Son, it's time you joined the Army of the Lord."

The man said, "Reverend, I've been a member of the Army of the Lord for years. I'm in church ready to battle against evil every Sunday."

The pastor was puzzled. "I'm sorry, but I've never seen you in church."

The man explained, "That's because I'm in camouflage."

Peter put a robe and a gray beard on the leader of his toy soldier troop. He called them "Moses and the Ten Commandos."

***

"ARE YOU SURE YOU DON'T WANT
TO HAVE A BIG FINISH?"

Deacon Tom used to be a weather reporter, which explains why his all-time favorite hymn is "Lo, He Comes with Clouds Descending."

***

The realtor's favorite hymn:

"I've Got a Mansion, Just over the Hilltop"

***

Please join us Saturday at 2:00 for our Annual Church Pot Lick. Details forthcoming!

"I don't think this milk is good," Mom told Billy.

"Maybe it needs to go to church," he replied.

Our church harp is making circles in the hardwood floor. Suggestions on how to get rid of these harp "O" marks are greatly appreciated.

✳✳✳

"I'M TAKING A HOLIDAY BREAK. INSTEAD OF PREACHING FIRE AND BRIMSTONE, I'M PREACHING SNOWFLAKES AND ICICLES."

Guarding the front of the nativity scene under the Christmas tree was a small armored figure with tape over its mouth. When asked who it was, Kyle said, "That's the silent knight!"

***

After setting up the manger scene, the congregation will join us in singing "The First Motel."

***

Father Ray's church was the last building before the lake and he was tired of all the people speeding past it on Sunday mornings to spend a day in the sun. He asked his local police officer for help. The police officer agreed that the traffic was a problem and put up a sign that read, "Slow, church."

A few weeks later he stopped by on Sunday morning and was pleased to see traffic slowed to a crawl and some people even pulling over and getting out. He saw Father Ray and said, "I guess my sign is working."

Father Ray shook his head. "Your sign didn't work at all so I put up my own." He led the officer to the front of the church where there was a large handwritten sign that read, "Slow, nude beach."

***

A note to the pastor:

Good news: Church attendance rose dramatically the last three weeks. Bad news: You were on vacation.

***

Dear God,
If you watch me in church this Sunday, make sure you check out my new shoes.

Mickey, age 8

"MY GOOGLE SEARCH CAME UP EMPTY.
I'M SEEKING FORGIVENESS."

Reverend Jack gets pretty frustrated with the teens in his Bible study class, especially when they ask if the e-pistles were e-mails from God.

***

The church bulletin can now be viewed online. If you do not have a computer, e-mail Margaret and ask her to forward it to you.

Melissa returned from Sunday school and reported, "Moses died before he reached Canada."

***

After attending Sunday school, Sarah informed her mother that Solomon had 300 wives and 700 porcupines.

***

"Why did Jesus choose 12 apostles?" the Sunday school teacher asked.

Ben speculated, "So his softball team would have a couple of extra pitchers?"

***

Due to the rector's illness, Wednesday night healing services will be discontinued until further notice.

***

The ladies of the church have cast-off clothing of every kind, and they can be seen in the church basement on Friday.

***

A sermon by the visiting minister will be followed by a luncheon: Attend and you will hear an excellent speaker and heave a great meal.

***

Please welcome Carl and Janet Kilpatrick to our congregation. Their telephone number is 555-436-8729, but they have requested that we keep this private.

"WHAT WOULD YOU THINK ABOUT
GETTING NEW HYMN BOOKS?"

The pastor was sitting in his office when one of his assistants came in with a problem.

"Where did you find the new organist?" the assistant asked.

The pastor was too ashamed to admit he met the man playing piano at a bar, so he said, "I don't remember at the moment. Why?"

"He had some strange songs to play with my Bible readings today. For the story of Daniel, he played 'The Lion Sleeps Tonight.' For David and Goliath, he played 'Everybody Must Get Stoned.' And for Methuselah, he played 'Stayin' Alive.'"

Dear God,
Of all the people who
worked for you, I like
Noah and David best.

Rob, age 7

***

Dear God,
Are you really invisible or is that just a trick?

Lucy, age 4

How does God know the good people from the bad people? Do you tell him, or does he read it in the newspapers?

Adam, age 6

***